Acknowledgments

This analysis of guaranteed issue and community rating laws and the consequences attending the implementation of these laws was not researched and written in a vacuum. Let me first recognize prime supporters in this effort.

Mr. Lee Tooman, vice president of government affairs for Golden Rule Insurance Co., shared with me volumes of supporting documentation and what seemed to me to be an unending supply of validated but unpublished research.

Dr. Merrill Matthews, director of the Council for Affordable Health Insurance (CAHI), which published a paper on community rating 10 years ago warning of an impending health insurance meltdown, was both an inspiration and ongoing resource for this book.

Mrs. Diane Bast, vice president, The Heartland Institute, and senior editor for this series of case studies, was a taskmaster, making sure that I wrote clearly, presented ideas concisely and, most importantly, dealt with the facts accurately. I also thank Joseph Bast, president of The Heartland Institute and publisher of *Health Care News*, for providing me the wherewithal to be associated with this project.

A tip of the hat goes to numerous state legislators who provided a perspective to this series that would have been missing without their willingness to share some of their valuable time for an interview.

Other reviewers who made a significant contribution include Victoria Craig Bunce, CAHI director of research and policy; J.P. Wieske, CAHI director of state affairs; and Michael Phillips, also with CAHI.

Adam Brackemyre, executive director of the Coalition Against Guaranteed Issue, always seemed to be there when I had a question, and he always had the right answer. Adam also took a run at the entire draft for this book. If there are any remaining errors, they are mine alone.

My wife, Dr. C. Zoe Smith, professor in the School of Journalism at the University of Missouri, deserves pages of credit for sustaining me during late nights and countless re-writes, and for understanding my occasional lapses of gratitude.

Finally it all boils down to this: I also owe a debt to the insurance professionals cited in this series and to many others who offered counsel and remain nameless, but not forgotten. They are all members of the highly regarded National Association of Health Underwriters. They provided me with leads and a clear vision of what can happen when legislators force poorly crafted social policy upon their constituents and then fail to undo the damage.

— Conrad F. Meier

Publishers' note: Conrad F. Meier died unexpectedly on March 18, 2005 of injuries sustained after a stroke. We have lost a dear friend and valued colleague. The publication of this book, to which he devoted so much time and energy and spirit, is dedicated to his memory, and to the cause of free-market health care reform that meant so much to him.

Preface

Between February and October of 2004, *Health Care News* featured a series of monthly case studies documenting how guaranteed issue and community rating laws have destroyed the individual health insurance market in eight states.[1] These mandates are not merely poorly crafted laws; they undermine what should be a voluntary, thriving, consumer-driven insurance marketplace. They have succeeded only in making individual health insurance coverage more expensive and less available than it otherwise would have been. As a result, hundreds of thousands of people have been shut out of the health insurance market in these states.

With the exception of Kentucky and New Hampshire, where policymakers are attempting to restore the free market and individual choice, the states profiled have done little to address the serious damage their 1990s' interventions have caused. It remains to be seen whether elected officials in Maine, Massachusetts, New Jersey, New York, Vermont and Washington will move in the direction of a more consumer-driven health care marketplace by taking our recommendations to heart. It is not too late to act. Specifically, we urge state policymakers in states with guaranteed issue to:

- Repeal guaranteed issue and community rating laws;
- Roll back mandated insurance benefits by allowing insurers to offer "mandate-lite" and even mandate-free policies;
- Give individuals who buy insurance the same tax breaks as those whose employers provide insurance;

---

[1] Because these were news articles, they did not include footnotes when they originally appeared. However, we have added a list of important resources at the end of the book.

- Encourage the use of Health Savings Accounts by giving public employees and those in high-risk pools the option to choose them and providing state income tax deductions for deposits made to the accounts;
- Permit more health insurance options, including policies sold through membership in associations.

— Joseph L. Bast
President, The Heartland Institute
Publisher, *Health Care News*

Introduction

During the early 1990s, state legislators and insurance regulators faced growing public concern over two health insurance problems. The first was rising insurance premiums, in part the result of increased utilization but also because a growing number of state-imposed mandates and restrictions on managed care practices threatened to price middle- and low-income consumers out of the private insurance market. The second was "job lock," the inability of people to take their health insurance with them when they changed jobs.

Each state adopted a different package of legislation and reforms. Some created high-risk pools that subsidized the premiums of people with health problems that made them uninsurable; some passed tort reform to reduce the cost of unnecessary litigation; some offered tax credits to the uninsured and unemployed.

Several states adopted regulations requiring health insurance companies to accept anyone who applied for coverage and charge everyone within each group the same rates regardless of their age, gender, lifestyle choices or health status. These regulations, called guaranteed issue and community rating respectively, were intended to force healthy people to subsidize less-healthy people, younger people to subsidize older people, and to make it easier for people without health insurance—especially those with a pre-existing medical condition—to get back into the system.

Eight states—Kentucky, Maine, Massachusetts, New Hampshire, New Jersey, New York, Vermont and Washington—imposed guaranteed issue and community rating laws on health insurance companies that sold to individuals as well as to small groups. That legislation, controversial at the time, has had a devastating impact on the health insurance marketplaces in those states.

Early Warning

In 1993, when guaranteed issue and community rating were first imposed on the individual health insurance markets in New Jersey, New York and Vermont, a study produced by the Council for Affordable Health Insurance (CAHI) warned the mandates would make the problems of high insurance premiums and lack of access to insurance worse, not better.

"Most of today's uninsured are young and do not have much money," the CAHI report said. "Community rating forces them to subsidize the cost of the middle-aged, who are at their peak earning power. Forcing the young to pay more will drive them out of the insurance market, raising costs for everyone."

Using a sophisticated health database called SimuCare, the authors showed how community rating would work in practice. Starting with a normal population of 100,000 people, the study predicted that eventually 31,500 people—mostly younger and lower-income—would drop their insurance coverage because of higher prices. Approximately 10,000 older and less-healthy people would buy insurance. With fewer people to share the cost and with higher expected health costs, premiums would have to go up by about 25 percent, according to the SimuCare model. That increase would come on top of the rate increases caused by inflation, cost shifting, increased utilization and other trends.

The CAHI report did not address guaranteed issue. If it had, it would have found similar results. Guaranteed issue laws increase the average age of the insurance pool and attract sicker people to it. Insurance premiums have to go up to subsidize the newcomers because they tend to have (sometimes serious) medical conditions, just as community rating forces the young to subsidize the middle-aged and near-elderly.

"Community rating will not work to extend coverage" to the currently uninsured, the CAHI study concluded, "because, as predominantly young, low-income people, they have difficulty allocating scarce dollars to insurance premiums. Additionally, it is precisely this population that experiences the biggest premium increases from going from risk-based premium rates to community-rated premiums."

Ten Years Later

Today, some 10 years later, it is possible to put CAHI's predictions to the test. What has happened to individual insurance markets in the eight states that adopted community rating and/or guaranteed issue beginning in 1992 and 1993? The data tell a grim story:

- Between 1994 and 2003, the share of the population in these eight guaranteed issue states covered by individual health insurance plans fell dramatically.
- The eight states have seen a massive exodus of private insurance companies that had been selling individual health insurance policies. Some 45 insurers, for example, left Kentucky between 1994 and 1997.
- Premiums for individual insurance have soared. In Maine, for example, the monthly premium for a family policy for someone aged 25 ranges from $1,270 to $2,388.
- By contrast, states that did not adopt guaranteed issue and/or community rating have seen much smaller premium increases. For example, typical monthly insurance premiums for families in rural counties in Vermont are approximately five times as much as they are for families in rural counties in Illinois.

Eight Case Studies

Starting with New Jersey, this analysis presents eight case studies, documenting how guaranteed issue and community rating have destabilized and sometimes destroyed the private individual insurance markets in states that adopted such legislation. The case studies offer an overview of legislative activity, data on uninsured rates and participation in the individual insurance marketplace[2], and premium costs for typical families.

The case studies also provide comments from individuals, small business owners, business and civic leaders, elected officials, and regulators giving their own perspectives on what has happened during the past decade. We also analyze alternatives to guaranteed issue and community rating where they've been tried.

The lesson from this series is clear: Imposing guaranteed issue and community rating laws on the individual health insurance market causes premiums to rise, not fall, and makes it more difficult, not easier, for the uninsured to find affordable coverage.

Key Definitions

Guaranteed issue (GI) laws forbid health insurance companies from denying coverage to anyone who applies for health insurance, including those individuals who apply for insurance after the onset of a chronic health condition or who have made lifestyle choices known to be unhealthy. Adopted to help end "job lock," GI has the unintended consequence of encouraging people to wait until they get sick before buying health insurance, which increases the number of uninsured and the premium costs for those who remain insured.

Pure **community rating** (CR) laws require health insurance companies to charge the same premium to everyone, regardless of age, sex, health history, lifestyle choices and regional demographics. This one-size-fits-all approach results in charging young and healthy people higher premiums than their expected medical expenses would justify in order to subsidize costs for middle-aged, older and less-healthy people.

Under "modified" CR, premium variations are allowed to compensate for certain risk characteristics such as age, sex and family size, but not for others such as health status or lifestyle choices.

---

[2] Some Census data and statistics are updated from the original publication of the series. Premium rates cited in the book were current in Spring 2005.

1

New Jersey

Welcome to New Jersey, where people with individual health insurance pay more than $12,000 a year for premiums and can spend as much as $263,904 (though we don't suppose anyone actually pays that much).

Thanks to regulations passed in 1992, New Jersey has some of the highest insurance premiums in the entire country and an individual health insurance industry that is on life support. New Jersey legislators have passed many health insurance laws during the past decade, mostly to fix problems caused by the original 1992 reforms. But there is little evidence policymakers are willing to reexamine the flawed policies that have wrecked the state's health insurance industry and robbed its customers of their freedom to choose affordable policies.

Legislative History

In 1992, New Jersey Blue Cross and Blue Shield (NJBCBS) was the state's "insurer of last resort," meaning it was required to provide health coverage—known as guaranteed issue—in the individual market to persons who did not qualify for group coverage or Medicare or Medicaid. Some 175,000 persons were insured in 1992 by NJBCBS under individual plans.

According to one estimate, NJBCBS lost $20 million on its individual insurance policies in 1992 but received subsidies to offset its losses, financed by a surcharge on hospital rates. In May 1992, a federal court ruled the surcharges violated the Employee Retirement Income Security Act of 1974 (ERISA), a federal law that preempts state intrusion into employer-based, self-funded health plans. Although that ruling was subsequently reversed, NJBCBS at the time feared the loss of its subsidy and had been lobbying for legislative relief even before the court decision.

The result was the Individual Health Coverage Program, requiring insurance carriers doing business in New Jersey to either offer individual health insurance on a guaranteed issue basis or pay an assessment to carriers that did. Other elements of the legislation were:

- Guaranteed coverage for all eligible people regardless of their health status (though a pre-existing condition exclusion allows insurers to limit coverage benefits to medical care not related to the pre-existing condition during the first 12 months);
- Guaranteed renewal of policies, provided (1) the insured does not become eligible for coverage under a group plan; (2) premiums are paid in a timely fashion; and (3) no fraud is committed by the insured;
- Community rating of the premiums, with variation allowed only for family status (single, adult plus child, husband and wife, and family); and
- Standardized insurance plans, referred to as Plans A, B, C, D and, at the time, E, all indemnity options, and a single HMO plan. (See New Jersey Figure 1 for coverage details.)

Skyrocketing Premiums

According to John A. Kalosy, the New Jersey legislative chairman for the National Association of Health Underwriters, "Community rating linked with standard state-mandated plan designs was like mixing nitrogen and glycerin and expecting it not to blow up."

Monthly premiums for family coverage under "Plan D" ($500 deductible, indemnity insurance) offered in New Jersey by Aetna rose from $769 in 1994 to $6,025 in 2005, a stunning 683 percent increase. An increase by NJBCBS was similar. (See New Jersey Figure 2.)

New Jersey Figure 1
Coverage Under Standard Plans Required by the New Jersey Individual Health Coverage Program

Plan	Plan A/50	Plan B	Plan C	Plan D	HMO
Coverage	Medical & Hospital	Medical & Hospital	Medical & Hospital	Medical & Hospital	Medical & Hospital
Carrier/ Covered Person Coinsurance	50%/ 50%	60%/ 40%	70%/ 30%	80%/ 20%	Carriers have the option to cover drugs at 50%
Deductible/ Copayment Options	$1,000/ $2,500	$1,000/ $2,500	$1,000/ $2,500	$500/ $1,000	$10/$15/ $20/$30
Hospital Confinement Copay	No	Yes-In addition to deductible	No	No	No

Source: http//www.state.nj.us/dobi/bgihc98.htm#DESCRIP (June 2005).

As of June 2005, the annual premium cost for a family Plan D policy from Aetna was an incredible $72,300. The cost of similar coverage from other carriers wasn't any better: $89,424 for NJBCBS, for example.

The carriers in New Jersey Figure 2 were chosen because they have sold Plan D policies since 1994. They were neither the most expensive nor the least expensive insurers in New Jersey. In 1994, however, according to the New Jersey Department of Banking and Insurance, there were about 14 carriers operating in the market. As of June 2005, there were only a handful left with only two carriers, Aetna and NJBCBS, operating since 1994. In 1995, Celtic entered the market and by 1996 was charging $798 per month. As of June 2005, Celtic charged an amazing $21,992 a month—$263,904 a year!

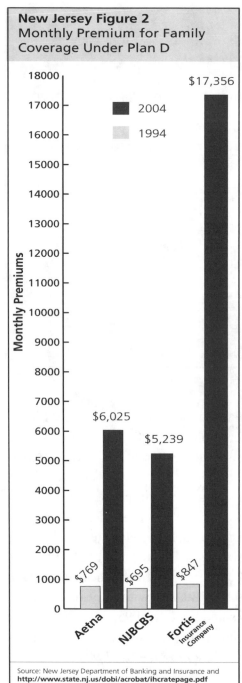

New Jersey Figure 2
Monthly Premium for Family Coverage Under Plan D

- 2004
- 1994

Monthly Premiums

$17,356

$6,025

$5,239

$769 $695 $847

Aetna NJBCBS Fortis Insurance Company

Source: New Jersey Department of Banking and Insurance and
http://www.state.nj.us/dobi/acrobat/ihcratepage.pdf
(June 2005).

The lowest monthly premium for a family Plan D policy (i.e., $500 deductible), as of June 2005 was $3,912 offered by Oxford. New Jersey Figure 3 shows the lowest monthly premiums charged for each of the four indemnity plans and the HMO plan required under the Individual Health Coverage Program. The lowest rate in the table is $468/month ($5,616/year) for PPO coverage for a single individual (not family) with a $1,000 deductible.

"New Jersey state legislators are unable or unwilling to cut benefits out of the standard plans because of perceived political pressure," says Kalosy. "The average consumer is unable to afford the high cost of the individual health plans."

Declining Coverage

The second impact of the 1992 reforms was a dramatic decline in the number of people who have individual health insurance. Exactly how many people buy individual health insurance in New Jersey is controversial, but data from three sources all show a rapid decline. (See New Jersey Figure 4.)

- According to U.S. Census Bureau data, the number of persons in New Jersey with individual health insurance fell from 998,000 in 1994 to 623,000 in 2003.

New Jersey Figure 3
Lowest Monthly Premiums for Individual Health Insurance in New Jersey

Plan	Status	Deductible/ Lowest Copay	Monthly Rate	Carrier
A	Single	$1,000	$517	Oxford
A	Adult + Child	$1,000	$957	Oxford
A	Two Adults	$1,000	$1,035	Oxford
A	Family	$1,000	$1,474	Oxford
B	Single	$1,000	$756	Aetna
B	Adult + Child	$1,000	$1,299	Aetna
B	Two Adults	$1,000	$1,513	Aetna
B	Family	$1,000	$2,055	Aetna
C	Single	$1,000	$468	Oxford PPO
C	Adult + Child	$1,000	$866	Oxford PPO
C	Two Adults	$1,000	$937	Oxford PPO
C	Family	$1,000	$1,335	Oxford PPO
D	Single	$500	$1,373	Oxford
D	Adult + Child	$500	$2,540	Oxford
D	Two Adults	$500	$2,745	Oxford
D	Family	$500	$3,912	Oxford
HMO	Single	$15	$494	NJBCBS
HMO	Adult + Child	$15	$757	NJBCBS
HMO	Two Adults	$15	$1,056	NJBCBS
HMO	Family	$15	$1,496	NJBCBS

Source: http://www.state.nj.us/dobi/acrobat/ihcratepage.pdf (June 2005).

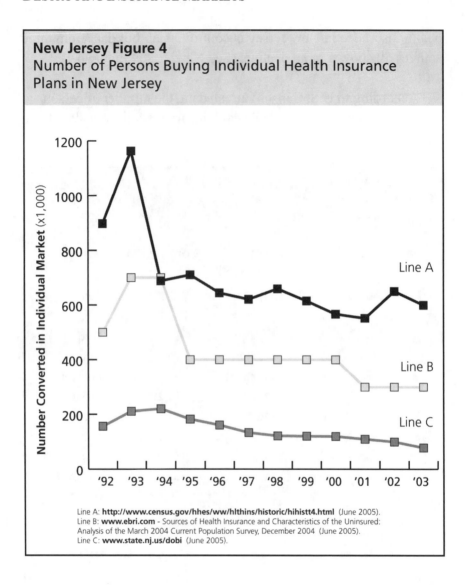

New Jersey Figure 4
Number of Persons Buying Individual Health Insurance Plans in New Jersey

Line A: **http://www.census.gov/hhes/ww/hlthins/historic/hihistt4.html** (June 2005).
Line B: **www.ebri.com** - Sources of Health Insurance and Characteristics of the Uninsured:
Analysis of the March 2004 Current Population Survey, December 2004 (June 2005).
Line C: **www.state.nj.us/dobi** (June 2005).

- According to the Employee Benefits Research Institute, which excludes persons age 65 and older from its estimates, the number of people with individual coverage fell from 500,000 in 1992 to an average of 300,000 between 2001 and 2003.
- Finally, the New Jersey Individual Health Coverage Program

estimates the number of individual insurance policies fell from 156,565 in 1993 to 78,298 in 2003.

Thus, depending on the data used, there has been a 40 to 50 percent decline in insurance coverage since New Jersey passed its legislation.

Fleeing Carriers

The third impact of the 1992 reforms has been a decrease in the number of insurance carriers willing to sell individual insurance in New Jersey. Until a few years ago, proponents of the 1992 reforms maintained the program worked. In mid-1999, for example, Katherine Swartz (Harvard School of Public Health) and Deborah Garnick (Brandeis University) referred to the program as an "unprecedented achievement." To justify their praise, they claimed that in 1995, 28 carriers were serving the New Jersey individual market with guaranteed issue products (more than the 14 carriers selling Plan D policies cited by the Department of Banking and Insurance).

By December 2003, however, only 15 carriers served the market. Even this number overstates the amount of competition in the market. Counting only carriers with distinct corporate parents reduces the number of firms to 11. And the very high premiums charged by some companies suggest they are filing rates but not selling polices.

Why companies pulled out is not difficult to understand. Guaranteed issue means people with chronic illnesses cannot be turned down for individual health insurance coverage, even though by traditional underwriting standards they are uninsurable. Community rating means carriers are forced to set their premiums sufficiently high to cover these "worst case" customers, making their policies unaffordable to virtually anyone else. The result is a "death spiral" of ever-rising premiums and "adverse selection," where the healthy drop their coverage and only those with poor health and high medical expenses choose to buy individual insurance.

Making an already bad situation worse, in 1996 insurance companies were assessed $43.5 million to offset the losses of

NJBCBS. By August of that year, NJBCBS had been reimbursed $81.5 million for its losses in the individual market. If anyone benefited from the 1992 legislation, it was NJBCBS. Most of its competitors have been driven out of business or out of the state.

Trying to Repair the Damage

Additional new regulations soon followed, prompted largely by market responses to the 1992 and 1994 regulations. In 1998, following public complaints about the quality of managed care, a law was enacted to regulate HMO conduct. In 1999, following the high-profile bankruptcy of Garden State, an indemnity insurer, regulators were given greater authority over insurer solvency. In 2000, legislation was passed to bail out two bankrupt HMOs.

In 2001, more legislation was adopted targeting HMO conduct, this time making external panel recommendations mandatory and giving private consumer groups ombudsmen-like authority over HMOs. Legislation adopted in 2002 created a "Basic and Essential Coverage" plan stripped of some mandates and the community rating standard (though rates are still regulated, there is some variation due to such factors as age, sex and geography). However, the plans do not appear to be selling well.

In November 2003, then-New Jersey Gov. James McGreevey (D) signed legislation creating a Mandated Health Benefits Advisory Commission to study the "social, financial, and medical impact of proposed mandated health benefits." The 15-member commission will review any proposed legislation that would require health insurance carriers to provide specific health benefits.

Conclusion

It has been more than 10 years since New Jersey legislated sweeping changes to its individual health insurance code. The combination of guaranteed issue and community rating has nearly destroyed the health insurance market for individuals.

Most of the new laws adopted since 1994 have failed to address the real sources of the damage caused by the state's sweeping 1992 insurance regulations. Instead, these subsequent laws battle the unintended consequences of bad policies, such as bankruptcies, rising premiums, and unaccountable and financially unstable HMOs.

Lawrence Koller, an independent insurance broker in Northern New Jersey and a member of the National Association of Health Underwriters, says "a major problem is that no politician wants to face these issues. No one wants to take away benefits. In fact, if a politician is sitting in his/her office and a constituent comes in complaining their insurance doesn't cover something, the politician is more likely to try to help the constituent by offering a new mandate that the health plan has to cover. The impact on rates and potential future 'uninsured' doesn't seem to be given as much weight."

Koller goes on to say, "The media don't help either. The typical news report doesn't distinguish between large group, small group, and individual insurance markets. The public and politicians lump all insurance companies together as the bad guys—the ones with the deep pockets."

Enactment in 2002 of the "Basic and Essential Coverage" plans with fairly broad rate bands is a small but favorable step back from the abyss. The legislation recognizes the need to allow carriers to offer individual health insurance plans that are attractive to the young and healthy. It seeks to accomplish this, though, by allowing insurers to offer deliberately crippled insurance products that the chronically ill will not want to buy. New Jerseyans deserve affordable individual health insurance policies without being forced to settle for policies that expose them to a minimum out-of-pocket cost (not including premiums) of $6,000 per year.

Unfortunately, there seems to be little interest among New Jersey legislators in abandoning the community rating and guaranteed issue mandates that have caused the state's insurers and their customers so much suffering. Until that attitude changes, New Jersey will remain the "poster child" for how to destroy a health insurance market.

2

Vermont

Former Vermont Gov. Howard Dean (D), a physician and unsuccessful candidate for the Democratic presidential nomination, considers his state a model for health care reform.

"In Vermont, where I served as governor for the last 11 years, nearly 92 percent of adults now have [health insurance] coverage," boasted Dean's campaign Web site. "Most importantly, 99 percent of all Vermont children are eligible for health insurance and 96 percent have it."

Universal health care—more accurately, universal health insurance—has been a Dean rallying cry for more than a decade. In 1992, his first year as governor, Dean pushed through to passage Act 160, which created the Vermont Health Care Authority, and charged it with bringing forth two sweeping health care reforms: a single-payer plan Dean had championed in 1991 as lieutenant governor and a measure he dubbed "regulated multi-payer."

Dean's effort to make health insurance universally available in Vermont has in many ways backfired. What has really become "universal" in the state are high health insurance premiums and a heavy tax burden needed to support the growing number of Vermonters covered not by private insurance, but by government-run Medicaid. Moreover, the number of uninsured Vermonters has increased, not fallen, since Dean's reforms took effect.

Legislative Mischief

In 1991, the Vermont Legislature passed Act 52, mandating guaranteed issue and community rating of insurance policies issued in the small group market. This caused young, healthy worker groups to face startling increases in premiums, since their age could no longer be taken into account in determining their risk. Many small businesses dropped their subsequently unaffordable health coverage and sent their employees to buy policies in the individual market. To close this "loophole," the Legislature followed up with Act 160 in 1992, extending the guaranteed issue and community rating mandates to insurers offering policies in the individual market.

By law, insurers are prohibited from using medical underwriting to set premiums. As permitted by law, the state's insurance commissioner initially permitted commercial insurers to deviate from community-rated premiums by 20 percent, but did not permit Blue Cross Blue Shield (BCBS) or Community Health Plan (CHP), the state's original nonprofit HMO, to deviate. For several years, BCBS lobbied for a change in the regulation. Effective January 1, 2000, the commissioner eliminated the rate deviation for all newly sold policies and phased out the deviation on all existing policies for the few remaining carriers.

More Uninsured

Guaranteed issue and community rating have wreaked havoc on Vermont's small group and individual insurance markets, just as they have in states across the country. The percentage of the state's population that is uninsured has actually increased since the mandates were imposed; premium rates have increased; and more Vermonters than ever are having to settle for government-run Medicaid in order to get insurance. Vermont is now second in the nation, after Tennessee, in the proportion of its under-65 population covered by Medicaid (21 percent).

Dean boasts that the share of Vermont's population without insurance fell during his tenure. In June 2000, an 11-member panel of state officials reported the percentage of the state's population that was uninsured had fallen from 10.8 percent in 1993 to 6.8 percent in 1997.

But those figures do not square with statistics compiled by the

U.S. Census Bureau. In an Ethan Allen Institute commentary (November 19, 2002), John McClaughry, the group's president and a member of the Vermont Senate between 1989 and 1992, noted, "According to Census Bureau figures, [the uninsured rate in Vermont] has gone from 9.5 percent (1992) to 9.7 percent (averaged over 1999-2001). In 1994 ... that data series ranked Vermont second in number of uninsured among the states. The 2001 ranking for health insurance coverage placed Vermont 10th in the nation."

McClaughry acknowledges that due to the small sample size used by the Census Bureau's Current Population Survey (CPS), estimates of the uninsured population can vary widely from year to year. In defending his Medicaid expansion in 1997, however, Dean touted his state's high ranking (second in 1994). The 1995 CPS, however, had dropped Vermont to 23rd. Dean did not acknowledge the new ranking.

Insurers Leave

According to State Rep. Frank Mazur (R-South Burlington), "Former Gov. Dean's community rating and guaranteed issue policy initiatives have driven out private insurers from Vermont."

About 25 percent of Vermont's private health insurance market—about 18,000 people in the individual market and 33,000 in the small group market—is subject to community rating. The remaining 75 percent of the market—associations, large groups and self-insured companies—has premiums based on health underwriting and experience rating.

What was formerly a healthy and affordable individual and small group health insurance market boasting 33 competitive insurance companies is now a shell of its former self. Such highly regarded companies as Aetna, Fortis, Golden Rule Insurance, Kaiser Permanente, Nationwide, Trustmark and, most recently, Mutual of Omaha, have all left a market known to be a hostile environment in which to do business.

Today the only significant player in the individual health

insurance market is BCBS. In 2004, BCBS had 56 percent of the market (114,000 lives) and MVP Health Plan, Inc. had 19 percent (35,000 lives) of the market.

The Legislature clearly anticipated most insurance companies would abandon the state when it legislated guaranteed issue and community rating in 1992. As carriers left Vermont, their insureds became eligible for a "safety net" established by the Legislature. The safety net's key provisions:

- Health insurance must be made available to persons whose "insurer withdraws from the marketplace in Vermont."
- BCBS is required to provide safety net coverage at "substantially similar terms and prices" as what the insured originally had.
- "Substantially similar prices" is defined as prices identical to those paid by the insured during the preceding year, adjusted for trend by an amount up to 15 percent. The legislation also allows additional annual adjustments of up to 15 percent, provided the insurer offering the safety net coverage has at least an 80 percent loss ratio. Finally, the insurance commissioner is authorized by the legislation to permit an additional 15 percent increase if BCBS would be hurt without it.

For Whose Protection?

The legislative "safety net," alleged to be for the protection of Vermont's insured, appears to have worked more in favor of BCBS.

In early 1994, BCBS reported it would face a $6.2 million loss in 1994. Its surplus was down to $8.8 million, $7.1 million of which was its home office real estate.

BCBS reported that its loss ratio for the safety net business for 1994 was 88.4 percent. Insurance industry analysts say that, allowing for a reasonable administrative load, the company likely had a profit on its safety net business. But BCBS reported an underwriting loss of $1.4 million. It reported administrative costs twice that permitted by law. It then used a trend of 19 percent (unsupported in its rate filing with the state) to justify a rate increase of 37 percent for the safety net business.

State officials approved that increase in August 1995—apparently allowing BCBS to use the safety net business to subsidize losses in its own business.

Premiums Rise

"In 1992, nearly everyone (except the insurance industry) held the euphoric belief that 'reforming' health insurance would be a piece of cake," wrote Ted Cote in the *St. Albans Messenger* on August 21, 1995. "The fact that Vermont is still wistfully enamored with a socialist/single-payer scheme will likely guarantee continued failure."

Things have gone from bad to worse since Cote made his prediction in 1995. According to Mazur, "a high-deductible ($3,500) individual insurance policy for a 33-year-old in Vermont currently costs $379 a month. (In South Carolina, by contrast, it's $61 a month for a $2,000 deductible.) Differences in population are a minor factor but community rating and guaranteed issue are major impediments to health insurance costs in Vermont compared to other states."

There is also significant variance in the cost of family health insurance plans. In a 2001 article for *Health Care News*, Mazur reported that in Pennsylvania a family plan with a $1,000 deductible cost $190 a month; in Connecticut it was $230 a month. In Vermont, such a policy would cost more than twice as much, $543 a month.

"Insurance premiums are sky high," writes physician David Gratzer, a senior fellow at the Manhattan Institute, in the January 12, 2004 issue of *The Weekly Standard*. "'I'm paying a lot and getting little choice,' a self-employed Burlington resident told me. He wasn't kidding: to cover his wife and himself, he pays $5,000 a year for a plan with a $1,000 deductible. Because most carriers have left the state, there are only a few insurance companies left in business."

Shift to Taxpayers

The premium increases led many younger Vermonters to drop their private-sector insurance coverage. Dean-administration reformers stepped in, extending eligibility for Medicaid to a wider swath of the state's population. The program has been expanded to the point where children in a family of four earning three times the federal poverty level (now around $52,000) can get "free" health care from the state. The Dean administration actively promoted government coverage, urging parents to take their children off their private insurance and enroll them in the state program. Medicaid in Vermont has become a health care welfare program for the middle class.

According to Mazur, Dean's "attempt for a 'universal' health care solution further expanded Medicaid to almost 25 percent of our population." McClaughry notes, "Eleven Dean years have now gone by. The state share of Medicaid spending has risen from $86.7 million to $263.5 million." Medicaid is a joint state-federal program, and federal taxpayers pay about $458 million for Vermont's generosity.

In the spring of 2002, the state's Joint Fiscal Office projected the state Medicaid plan will be $42 million in the hole by 2006, even with no new beneficiaries. In his January 2004 budget message, Gov. Jim Douglas (R), Dean's successor, announced that if no corrective action is taken, the Medicaid deficit would come to $245 million by 2009.

Some observers have suggested Vermont's shift from private sector to government-run insurance was not an "unintended" consequence of the Dean reforms at all. "The root cause of Vermont's problem came in the late 1980s," explained McClaughry, "well before the Dean era, when Blue Cross Blue Shield of Vermont was threatened with insolvency. It used all of its political muscle to impose community rating and guaranteed issue on its competitors, who were taking away their customers.

"The competitors then obligingly departed the state," McClaughry continued. "Now, liberals stoutly defend a regressive single-payer health care system, managed by Blue Cross Blue Shield as a ward of the government."

In a 1995 letter to the *Hartford Courant*, Wallingford, Vermont resident John McTaggart wrote, "Instead of being rewarded for initiative and healthy choices, I have to be thrown in with a pool of many who did not conduct their health care and lifestyle in a manner similar to my own pursuits. Truth is the state wants individuals like myself to subsidize the rest of policyholders, and the way to get this done was to close the doors to insurance companies that rewarded better risk applicants."

Lawmakers in Denial

As the 2004 legislative session got underway in Vermont, some lawmakers continued to turn a blind eye toward the health insurance meltdown that has resulted from the state's misguided public policy actions.

State Sen. Rod Gander (D-Windham) told the *Brattleboro Reformer*, "Preserving Vermont's community rating law is a priority this session." Several of his Democratic Party colleagues agreed. State Rep. Richard Marek (D-Newfane) maintains, "Community rating has worked well in Vermont, although it's far from perfect."

Jeffrey and Charlotte Tullar are among many of the state's health care reform tragedies. The Tullars say they "never dreamed the state's fling at health care reform would cause them to lose their health insurance." Two years after the guaranteed issue and community rating mandates were passed, the Tullars faced a 170 percent premium increase. Their health insurance premium would have been more than their mortgage.

McClaughry notes, "Dean's policy was to drive out insurance companies, make ever more people dependent on government health care, underpay the providers, and replace personal responsibility with 'delivery of services.'"

Restoring the Free Market

The *Burlington Free Press*, the state's paper of record, editorialized in September 1995 that community rating had already failed and should be repealed. "It has the best of intentions, but has resulted in driving people who were paying their own way off insurance, and toward dependency on the state."

In its *2004 Position Statement on Health Care*, the Lake Champlain Regional Chamber of Commerce (LCRCC) encouraged policymakers to conduct a thorough review of the regulatory environment affecting the cost of health insurance in the state. The group also urged a movement away from community rating.

"It would be useful," stated the LCRCC, "to examine proposals for limited modifications in community rating. Some examples of modifications that could be looked at include allowing a 10 percent plus or minus rate band, geographic rating, industry rating or personal health accountability factors."

When Gov. Douglas was asked by reporters what measures he would implement to contain health insurance costs, he replied, "First, I would revisit community rating to create more flexibility and competition in the health insurance marketplace. I would instead have a high-risk pool to subsidize those Vermonters who are uninsurable. I would work to end the Medicaid cost shift that passes the high costs of this program onto consumers of private insurance. I would reduce unnecessary government mandates and move toward Medical Savings Accounts so employers and employees could contribute to a special tax-free account to pay for high-deductible, low-premium health insurance."

"Douglas also advocated providing more information to consumers and insurance discounts for healthy behavior," said Mazur, which would appear to be a step away from community rating. "Most of his policy recommendations are included in H 196 and a subsequent bill that I introduced this year."

If Vermont is going to back out of the mess it has made for itself, acknowledging that misguided public policies are to blame would seem to be an important first step. Repealing guaranteed issue and community rating mandates should be high on the reform agenda. Mandated insurance benefits, which needlessly raise the price of insurance, also should be rolled back. Giving individuals who buy insurance the same tax breaks as those whose employers provide insurance is yet another promising reform.

Vermonters also should consider additional reforms being entertained in other states, including a functional high-risk pool, to address the needs of the medically uninsured and uninsurable without skewing the insurance market for everyone else, and paying the reasonable charges of physicians, hospitals and other health care providers who provide services for the beneficiaries of state government health programs.

"I think many fear it's too much reform for the Democratically controlled state senate to accept," warned Mazur. Nevertheless, he acknowledged, small steps in the right direction are being made.

3
New York

In the early 1990s, Empire Blue Cross Blue Shield (BCBS) in New York was the largest private not-for-profit insurer in the nation. But its financial statements showed a company in serious trouble. It had violated state insurance regulations and pressed for enormous premium increases on individual policy holders, while at the same time selling health insurance polices below cost to major corporations and large employer groups.

Elizabeth McCaughey, Republican candidate for lieutenant governor at the time, described the situation in a September 1994 essay for the *Wall Street Journal*: "The financial statements [for Empire Blue Cross Blue Shield] complete a distressing picture drawn by the U.S. Senate Permanent Subcommittee on Investigations last year. Federal investigators concluded that Empire BCBS lacked the ability to 'properly execute the most basic functions of an insurance company.'"

As insurer of last resort for New York residents, BCBS sold community rated, guaranteed issue policies at state-regulated prices in exchange for an exemption from state and local income taxes. And it was allowed to pay hospitals lower prices for services than other commercial health insurers in the market were allowed to pay.

In Need of a Bailout

As premiums increased and financial problems continued to mount, it became clear BCBS needed some kind of bailout. When a for-profit company is poorly managed, the stockholders are the losers. When a nonprofit insurer is badly managed, it is the policyholders who get hurt.

Telling the Legislature it was about to lose more than

$438 million from combined underwriting losses in 1991 and 1992, BCBS lobbied for a whopping rate increase. The insurance commission approved an increase of 25.5 percent.

The situation implied to many legislators that further reforms were needed to control the entire health insurance market and protect BCBS from further losses. In 1993, they imposed guaranteed issue and community rating mandates on the state's individual and small group insurance markets. According to a *New York Times* report dated April 2, 1993, "BCBS maintained the new laws applying to private insurers would make the entire market more competitive."

The state's intervention in the insurance market affected not only insurance carriers and policyholders, but brokers and insurance agents as well. Insurance professionals are forbidden from selling or servicing individual health insurance policies in New York, even if the professionals are state-licensed and represent state-licensed health insurance companies that offer legitimate insurance policies. New Yorkers must purchase directly from an HMO or Healthy New York, the government-run insurance program.

Explained Patti Goldfarb, past president of the New York State chapter of the National Association of Health Underwriters, "If you are self-employed or you're an individual whose employer does not offer health insurance, your insurance options have been severely limited. There is no professional insurance support; your ability to research the available insurance companies is limited, and the ability to have someone advocate for you when claims are denied is greatly curtailed. This [fighting denial of claims] is a difficult undertaking for most individuals."

Premium Increases

"The New York version does not have a high-risk pool, does not allow age weighting, and disallows any medical underwriting," Goldfarb said. "Everyone has to be accepted at the same rate—healthy or not."

Mickey Lyons, downstate president of NAHU and Goldfarb's

partner at Medical Link, Inc., New York City, added, "The impact on health insurance premiums was enormous. Insurance underwriters recognized that the law now required them to assume greater unknown risks and were forced to increase premiums accordingly and significantly."

One month after the guaranteed issue and community rating laws went into effect, nearly 10 percent of the state's insured population experienced premium increases ranging from 20 to 59 percent. Rates for a 30-year-old single male increased by 170 percent. By June 2005, individual and family policy rates were higher still. (See New York Figure 1.)

"We are astounded," Senator Guy Velella (R-Bronx), a lead sponsor of the mandate bill, told the *New York Daily News* on March 10, 1993. "I don't know of one legislator who was prepared for the size of these [premium] increases. Consumers are outraged."

New York Figure 1
Average Annual Insurance Premiums in New York

	March '93 before Community Rating	March '93 after Community Rating		June 2005
Single Male Age 30	$1,200	$3,240	Individual Coverage	$4,452.60
Single Female Age 30	$1,800	$3,240		
Family Age 30	$4,020	$7,680	Husband/Wife Coverage	$8,786.91
Single Male Age 45	$2,520	$3,240		
Single Female Age 45	$2,640	$3,240	Family (2 parents with 1 child) coverage	$7,501.16
Family Age 45	$6,300	$7,680		
Single Male Age 60	$5,800	$3,240	Parent with 1 child coverage	$11,786.73
Single Female Age 60	$4,380	$3,240		
Family Age 60	$11,640	$7,680		

Source: **http://www.nyshmoguide.org/guides/2004GuideToHealthInsurers.pdf** (June 2005).

Toby McAfee, from Yonkers, was one of those outraged consumers. He wrote to the *New York Times* in August 1993, "My wife and I eat carefully, do not smoke, and exercise regularly. Are we paying health insurance premiums based on the poor health habits of others under the New York State law that mandates community rating rather than experience rating?"

In an answer that rings of Orwellian newspeak, John Calagna, a spokesman for the Department of Insurance, responded, "When it comes to health insurance, there are only two types of risks—poor risks and those that will become poor risks. It's a fact of life that as we grow older, our need for medical services intensifies."

Comparing Rates

A study released in September 2002 by the online health insurance brokerage eHealthInsurance puts New York's insurance rates into perspective. The study compared the cost of 20,000 policies, with 7,000 different benefit "mixes," issued in 42 states by more than 70 insurers, including large group plans offered by BCBS.

In California, which imposes neither guaranteed issue nor community rating on individual health insurance, the average holder of an individual policy paid an annual premium of $1,538. In Pennsylvania, the premium would be $1,656; in Texas, $1,596; and in Florida, $1,776. But in New York, eHealthInsurance reports that person would have paid $3,540 for similar benefits.

Data compiled by the Medical Expenditure Panel Survey (MEPS), a project of the Agency for Healthcare Research and Quality, finds New York to be the second most-expensive state in the country (behind Massachusetts) for family insurance offered in the small group market. At an average annual premium of $8,427.50, insurance in New York is 42 percent more expensive than in California and 48 percent more expensive than South Dakota, the lowest-cost state. (See New York Figure 2.)

New York Figure 2
Average Annual Insurance Premiums
Family Coverage through Small Groups

Highest Average Annual Premiums		Lowest Average Annual Premiums	
Massachusetts	$8,468.86	South Carolina	$6,083.00
New York	$8,427.50	Kansas	$6,041.64
New Hampshire	$8,290.90	Virginia	$6,009.21
New Jersey	$8,274.53	Iowa	$5,989.04
Connecticut	$7,597.89	California	$5,945.61
Maryland	$7,268.98	Mississippi	$5,901.51
Florida	$7,206.48	Kentucky	$5,894.18
Wisconsin	$7,134.04	Missouri	$5,790.45
Pennsylvania	$7,123.71	North Dakota	$5,713.15
Texas	$7,047.92	South Dakota	$5,678.65

Source: Medical Expenditure Panel Survey, Agency for Healthcare Research and Quality, 2000. **http://www.meps.ahrq.gov**

The Mutual Experience

Before guaranteed issue and community rating, Mutual of Omaha, one of the largest providers of individual indemnity health insurance policies in the state and the last to exit the market, charged a 25-year-old male on Long Island $81.64 a month. By contrast, a 55-year-old Long Islander buying the same policy paid $179.60.

Almost immediately after the mandates were passed, both residents paid a monthly premium of $135.95—a 67 percent increase for the 25-year-old and a 25 percent decrease for the 55-year-old. However, the older policyholder's gain at the expense of the younger was short-lived: by 1994, declining participation by younger people in the individual insurance market caused monthly premiums for males of both ages to reach $183.79. The 55-year-old was now paying more than he had before guaranteed issue and community rating.

By 1997, the monthly premium had risen to $217.59. Even more people dropped their individual health insurance polices, and many were forced to rely on charity health care, state government-run health plans and Medicaid.

More Uninsured

The New York Department of Insurance reported 43,666 individual policyholders canceled their insurance within 12 months of the mandates' effective date. The share of the state's population that was uninsured jumped from 20.9 percent in 1990 to 24.8 percent in 1995. The national average in 1995 was just 17.4 percent.

According to the actuarial firm Milliman, Inc., the mandates caused policy cancellations on a much greater scale than the Department of Insurance acknowledged. Milliman estimated 500,000 New Yorkers with individual and small group health insurance canceled their policies, reducing the number of insured from 2.8 million to 2.3 million. One of every six New Yorkers covered by individual or small group policies became uninsured as a result of the guaranteed issue and community rating laws.

In 1994, Mutual of Omaha reported that in 1993 it insured nearly 90,000 New Yorkers through individual plans. Fifteen months later, 43 percent of those policies had lapsed. All private insurance companies doing business in New York at the time had similar experiences.

More than half of those who dropped their policies, reported Mutual of Omaha, were under 35 years of age. The average age of those who renewed was 45. Forty-three percent of those who dropped a policy did not replace it with other coverage, becoming one more statistic in the state's uninsured population.

Between 1992 and 1993, Mutual of Omaha's claims cost doubled in New York. Nationally, the company's claims cost increased just 12 percent over that same period. More than 20 commercial indemnity companies, including Mutual of Omaha, either left New York entirely or stopped writing health insurance policies between

1993 and 2000. Competition in the industry became almost nonexistent, leading to continued double-digit premium inflation among the few carriers that remained.

According to U.S. Census Bureau figures, 11.7 percent of New York residents were insured in the individual market in 1994. By 2003, that share had fallen to just 7.4 percent. By comparison, in the U.S. roughly 12.0 percent of the population had individual coverage in 1994, falling to 9.2 percent by 2003.

Burden Shifts to Taxpayers

Health insurance reformers refused to admit, even after they were warned by policy experts, that the situation they faced was due primarily to the mandates they had passed earlier, with only a small part attributable to normal health care price inflation.

In 2000, alarmed by the increase to 3 million uninsured people in the state, the Legislature created a state-run health insurance bureaucracy called Healthy New York (HNY). Instead of repealing the mandates responsible for the situation, HNY would insure the uninsured at artificially low premiums subsidized by taxpayers. Between January 2001 and July 2003, taxpayer subsidies totaling $130 million were given to HNY.

To qualify for coverage under HNY, an applicant must:

- Have an annual income at or below 250 percent of the federal poverty line—about $50,000 for a family of four;
- Have been uninsured for the previous 12 months; and
- Not be eligible for private group insurance, Medicare or Medicaid.

New Yorkers covered by HNY pay premiums that are 50 percent of the market rate; taxpayers make up the difference.

The state was divided into nine geographical regions, with HNY being the primary, government-run subsidized health insurance option in all nine regions. The number of participating HMOs varies from three in Buffalo to 13 in the Long Island region. Different HMOs operate in different regions.

Premiums paid by those insured under HNY are community rated, although geographical variances are permitted. Annual rate increases up to 10 percent are permitted without approval from the Department of Insurance. Policies are subject to the guaranteed issue mandate, but the provider can impose a pre-existing condition limitation based on treatment or advice given up to six months before the policy's effective date.

"Finger in the Dike"

In an effort to make health insurance more affordable for the individual sole proprietor, the Legislature passed and the governor signed Sen. James Seward's (R-Otsego County) bill that redefined "small group." Before the measure passed, "small group" meant a group of 2 to 50 employees. With Seward's measure, "small group" now means 1 to 50 employees.

According to Elliott Shaw, director of government affairs for The Business Council of New York State, Inc., "This legislation allowed sole proprietors to continue to purchase individual health insurance [at small group rates]." Shaw also said that the legislation, while beneficial, was only a "finger in the dike." But even that assessment may be optimistic, because the legislation ultimately confuses group with non-group policies, trying to impose federal HIPAA legislation, intended for true group coverage, on the individual market.

Sun Rises on the HSA

Seward introduced a bill in the 2005 legislative session to formally recognize Health Savings Accounts (HSAs) as a legitimate consumer option in the New York market. By allowing consumers to purchase higher-deductible individual insurance plans, HSAs allow consumers to avoid some of the inflationary consequences of guaranteed issue and community rating. If Seward's measure passes, New Yorkers could find their HSA premiums significantly lower than what they currently can buy.

The New York Legislature also should consider the establishment of a workable high-risk pool in the state, which would address the needs of the medically uninsured and uninsurable without skewing the insurance market for everyone else.

Mandated insurance benefits, which needlessly raise the price of insurance, should also be rolled back, and the Legislature should consider—as other states have done, and as President George W. Bush has proposed—giving individuals who buy insurance the same tax breaks as those whose employers provide insurance.

4

Kentucky

On April 2, 2004, Kentucky Gov. Ernie Fletcher (R) signed HB 650, legislation aimed at resuscitating a health insurance market that has suffered greatly from a decade of state government interference.

The bill, titled simply "An Act Relating to Health Benefit Plans," passed the House of Representatives in March on a 95-2 vote and the Senate by 35-1. The measure will:

- Ban for three years all new state mandates requiring health insurers to cover specific medical conditions and treatments;
- Eliminate regulations that require all insurers to offer standard benefit plans; and
- Reduce bureaucratic paperwork and insurance rules to make them comparable to other states.

Observers hope the new law will encourage the return of many insurers who left the state after 1994. Currently, only Anthem Blue Cross Blue Shield, Humana, Fortis, John Alden, Mega Life and Health Insurance Company, and Physicians Mutual operate in Kentucky.

Unintended Consequences

In 1994, with the nation still abuzz over the Clinton administration's 1993 proposal to nationalize the country's health care system, the Kentucky Legislature passed sweeping measures policymakers believed at the time would make health insurance more affordable, and health care more accessible, for the state's residents.

The key provisions of HB 250 included guaranteed issue and modified community rating provisions; a risk-adjustment process among insurers that favored Blue Cross Blue Shield (BCBS); and five standard benefit plans that differed relatively little with respect to deductible and co-pay level. The benefit plans could not be amended until July 1995.

Policymakers also mandated the establishment of a statewide health purchasing alliance, known as Kentucky Kare. To ensure the plan's financial viability, policymakers required all state government employees to join. Kentucky Kare also served as the "insurer of last resort" for the uninsured not eligible for Medicaid.

The "reforms" were imposed on top of a complex system of consumer safeguards that included federal government requirements under the Consolidated Omnibus Budget Reconciliation Act (COBRA), mini-COBRA, benefit mandates, underwriting mandates, and financial reserve requirements. Little attention was paid by state legislators or the activists lobbying for the new mandates to potential interactions between the old and new regulations.

The combination of modified community rating, guaranteed issue, mandated benefit packages and patient access laws created contradictory and counter-productive incentives that hurt consumers, insurance companies and health care providers.

A 1996 law freezing premiums in the individual and small group markets at pre-reform rates made the mess even worse, while hiding the mounting problems from the general public. Healthy Kentuckians generally sought out policies with premium rates frozen at lower levels, while the unhealthy population was forced to choose between more expensive community-rated plans, Kentucky Kare or Medicaid.

Insurance Market in Turmoil

The new insurance industry regulations favoring BCBS and the mandate making government employees captive to Kentucky Kare had a devastating impact on the state's private individual and small group health insurance markets. In April 1997, the Kentucky Department of Insurance reported:

- By December 1996, 45 insurance companies had pulled out from the state's individual insurance market. Insurance Commissioner George Nichols told the *Louisville Courier-Journal* the state was "moving toward a crisis."
- Anthem BCBS—for years the state's largest insurer in the individual market and by 1996 virtually the only insurer—reported an underwriting loss of $60 million.
- Kentucky Kare reported a $30 million underwriting loss over the previous 20 months and so increased premiums 28 percent for 1996.

Premium Increases

As competition in Kentucky's individual insurance market fell and the few remaining insurers offered benefit packages mandated by the state, Kentuckians got a rude awakening. Out-of-pocket expenses rose above what they had been in pre-reform days, and average premiums jumped between 36 and 165 percent.

Donald Harden, a Florence insurance agent and president of the Northern Kentucky Association of Life Underwriters, reported at the time that one of his customers had been paying $380 a month for a family plan in the private insurance market. After the Legislature's 1994 actions, Harden's client had to buy into the Kentucky Kare plan for a monthly premium of $700, with reduced benefits.

The *Courier-Journal* reported on October 17, 1997, "Gail Collins, a self-employed food distributor in Louisville, said she had individual insurance but didn't think she should have to pay inflated premiums for the unhealthy.

"Steve Carter, owner of the 4th Avenue Deli, also in Louisville, is healthy but can't afford to buy insurance for himself and his seven employees," the *Courier-Journal* continued.

All told, some 850,000 Kentuckians faced dramatically higher premium payments after the 1994 reforms.

Increase in Uninsured Population

U.S. Census Bureau data suggest the Kentucky reforms may have resulted in an increase in the share of the state's population that was uninsured. In 1993, the year before the reform measure was passed, 12.5 percent of the state's population was uninsured. By 1996, that figure had reached 15.6 percent. It has since fallen again, to 14 percent in 2003, as attempts to undo the reforms have taken effect, but it remains higher than the pre-reform figure.

Fully 574,000 Kentuckians were without health insurance in 2003—a 22.6 percent increase over the 468,000 uninsured in 1993. By contrast, the number of people in the United States who were uninsured increased just 9.7 percent between 1993 and 2002.

In 1994, 12.0 percent of Kentucky's population was insured in the individual market, just under the national average of 13.1 percent. By 2001, the national average had fallen to 8.3 percent ... but in Kentucky, it fell even further. Just 6.9 percent of the state's population was insured in the individual market in 2001. (See Kentucky Figure 1.) However, as discussed below, in 2000 Kentucky decided to reform the reforms, returning to a more market-based system. As a result, individual coverage grew from 346,000 individual health insurance policies to 392,000 in 2003. About 9.5 percent of the Kentucky population was insured in the individual market in 2003—still below the 1994 number of 12 percent.

As Bob Rich, an independent insurance broker from Florence, told the *Kentucky Post* in April 1997, "The system was working for 95 percent of the people. We basically destroyed a system that works to satisfy the other 5 percent."

Not all Kentuckians agreed. In October 1997, a spokesperson for the Kentuckians for Health Care Coalition—an advocacy group that had lobbied hard for the 1994 legislation—told the *Courier-Journal*, "many Kentuckians with high-cost conditions today enjoy having insurance for the first time."

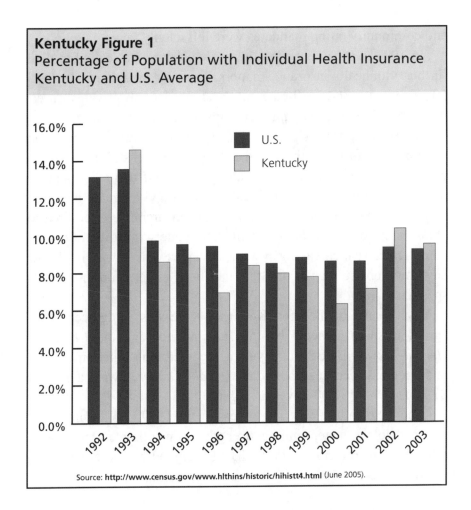

Kentucky Figure 1
Percentage of Population with Individual Health Insurance
Kentucky and U.S. Average

Source: http://www.census.gov/www.hlthins/historic/hihistt4.html (June 2005).

Reforming the Reforms

In 1996, the Legislature half-heartedly acknowledged the 1994 reforms weren't achieving the intended result. Realizing the state had become a magnet for unhealthy people from other states, policymakers imposed a one-year residency requirement for enrollment in Kentucky Kare. Other reforms allowed private insurance companies to exclude coverage of pre-existing conditions for 12 months, and the rating bands private insurers could charge were widened. Such "tweaking" notwithstanding, guaranteed issue and community rating mandates were left mainly intact.

In 1997, a special session of the Legislature was called to deal further with health insurance matters. The most notable result was a 50 percent rate increase for the state's near-monopoly private insurer; Anthem BCBS was pushing premiums to historic highs.

In 1998, legislators passed HB 315, a disastrously complicated attempt at reforming the reform. Insurers were still required to guarantee issue a standard plan along with their two most popular plans, more rating flexibility was approved and a streamlined rate review mechanism was put in place. But insurers were required to obtain state officials' approval of their underwriting practices. A complicated risk-spreading system was approved, as was a "play or pay" measure similar to one that had been rejected during 1997's special session.

By the end of the year, Kentucky Kare was being accused of "gross mismanagement" by the state auditor and the *Lexington Herald-Leader*. BCBS was saying it needed to raise rates an average of 52 percent because, reported the *Herald-Leader*, it was paying out $1.30 for every $1.00 it was taking in.

The Legislature was not in session in 1999. No insurers had returned to the state, lending strength to an ultimately successful effort toward reform in 2000. HB 517, signed by the governor in April that year, took many positive steps, including:

- Establishing a high-risk pool;
- Eliminating the guaranteed issue mandate; and
- Broadening the rate band, although keeping community rating in place.

The measure was not perfect, leaving in place certain regulations that ensured the state's climate for insurance carriers would remain less hospitable than other states. The five insurers that returned are a small share of the original 45 that once made up a vibrant and competitive insurance marketplace.

What the Future Holds

Golden Rule Insurance Co., now owned by UnitedHealth Group, told the *Courier-Journal* that Kentucky "has come a long way to restoring a market that is viable." While the company is weighing a decision to return, others will never return. Regulations adopted in Kentucky and in other states forced them out of the business of writing health insurance policies entirely.

"Kentucky's health insurance market is recovering from legislative changes made in 1994 and 1996 that inadvertently set the stage for declining competition, higher costs, and general insurance market instability," summarizes the Kentucky Chamber of Commerce in its *2003-04 Policy Document* on health care.

Nevertheless, the Chamber continues, "the fact that the state has 'reformed' health insurance every two years since the original reform in 1994 has created a climate which is not conducive for getting objective data about the right course of action for guiding the state out of the morass."

The measure recently signed by Gov. Fletcher that bans new mandated benefits, frees insurers from the standard benefit plan requirement, and cuts red tape and paperwork should make it easier for insurers to return to the state. Consumers, policy wonks, and insurance industry analysts will be watching closely. Kentucky may be on its way back from the abyss.

5
Washington

On March 31, Washington Gov. Gary Locke (D) signed into law HB 2460, an act that redefines a small group as any employer group with 2 to 50 employees. The small group reforms contained in HB 2460 only begin to undo policy failures adopted in the early 1990s by Washington State legislators and then-Gov. Mike Lowry (D).

Clinton-Care Reforms

In September 1993, Lowry signed the Washington Health Services Act (WHSA), a sweeping measure not unlike the Clinton administration's proposal to nationalize the country's health care system. Indeed, Lowry all but took credit for the Clinton plan, saying, "I am pleased President Clinton's reform proposals so closely resemble Washington State's new law."

State Representative Phil Dyer, ranking minority leader on the Health Care Committee at the time, said, "I watched the passage of a bill that was constantly being revised with [area code] 202 fax headers—the latest wisdom from Washington, DC—coming into the caucus, because in that Spring of 1993, the Ira Magaziner [health care] task force had been formed, and was, in fact, operating."

As if sending a warning to the rest of the nation, a solidly liberal Washington state Legislature eventually passed individual health insurance reform that included key elements of the original Clinton plan:

- Insurers were required to guarantee issue insurance;
- Insurers were required to offer a Basic Health Plan covering a government-defined set of benefits. Insurers were permitted to offer other plans, including plans with fewer benefits;

- Insurers were required to use a modified community rating scheme, allowing premium variations only for geography, age, family size, length of time with insurance from that company and wellness;
- Insurers were permitted to adjust premiums only annually, except in cases where the number of people in the insured's family or benefits choice changed, or if laws were passed that would affect premiums;
- Insurers were permitted to exclude coverage of pre-existing conditions for only 90 days prior to the effective date of insurance coverage; and
- The state department of insurance was given authority to approve or disapprove all insurance-related regulatory actions, including actions on rate increases, benefit designs, community rating parameters and guaranteed issue provisions.

Implementation

Implementation of the WHSA was left in the hands of Insurance Commissioner Deborah Senn. Washington is one of only a few states where the insurance commissioner is an elected position, and Senn's efforts on the WHSA initiative often seemed to reflect her need to "campaign" for popularity among voters.

Early in 1994, Senn and a group of insurance company officials announced at a news conference the first step of her plan: a three-month open-enrollment period beginning in July 1994. Any of the state's 600,000 uninsured residents could apply for individual insurance policies at community rates mandated by state law, which the insurers guaranteed they would issue. State actuaries estimated the reforms would raise overall insurance rates by only 3 to 5 percent, with no single insurer carrying the bulk of the cost.

The success of the WHSA hinged on the ability of insurers to spread the cost of the new enrollees, many of them considered high-risk for health insurance purposes, among the state's 4.4 million policyholders. To do that, Senn needed approval from the state

Legislature and a congressional waiver of regulations that would otherwise exclude from the state's cost-sharing program 1.4 million Washington residents whose employers were self-insured under ERISA.

During the open enrollment period, thousands of formerly uninsured Evergreen State residents signed up. With the prospect of thousands of new customers and only modestly higher costs, some insurers eagerly took advantage of open enrollment. One of the state's major insurers, Pierce County Medical Bureau Inc., began signing up enrollees several months before the official start of the program and added some 6,000 customers. Principal Mutual signed up 2,200 enrollees, increasing its roster of individual policyholders by more than a third.

Reforms Begin to Unravel

It wasn't long, though, before the WHSA began to unravel. In 1995, the state Legislature repealed most of the cost-sharing provisions that had made the WHSA palatable to the state's insurers. Legislators did not, however, lift the open enrollment provision or the guaranteed issue and community rating mandates.

With insurers' rolls over-flowing with new, often high-risk policyholders and no way to spread the cost, the bills began to pile up.

Pierce County Medical said its monthly medical costs for individual policyholders soared 67 percent in the first year to nearly $100 a month, up from about $60. Its 6,000 new policyholders cost even more—an average of $131 a month, according to John Holtermann, the company's chief operating officer. The company was paying about $1 million a month more in claims against individual policies than it was receiving in premiums.

Principal Mutual fared even worse. Its generous plan drew some of the highest-risk enrollees. By 1995, the Des Moines, Iowa insurer logged about $32 million in health insurance claims in Washington State alone, but raised just $20 million in premiums—nearly twice the average cost of its claims elsewhere in the U.S.

Insurers Seek Rate Increases

Insurers doing business in Washington's individual market began filing for big rate increases to cover the soaring costs. During the 1995-1996 rating period, Blue Cross of Washington and Alaska filed for a 19 percent increase for 80,000 individual policyholders. Pierce County Medical wanted a 34 percent boost on its individual policies. Rate increases were denied. Principal Mutual notified Senn's department it planned to stop writing individual health insurance policies altogether.

Senn said insurers deliberately tried to sabotage her efforts. Insurers denied the accusation, noting Senn threw open the state's insurance rolls before cost-sharing was in place. Rep. Dyer said of Senn, "She had no technical expertise in this area. She just wanted to rush in and make people happy."

Some state legislators tried to undo the damage. Republicans and Democrats alike offered bills during the 1996 session to raise funds to cover the spiraling health insurance claims. The bills were rejected.

As Bill Baldwin, president of the Washington Institute for Policy Studies, noted in 1997, "The market for individually-purchased health insurance in Washington is 'hemorrhaging,' 'bleeding,' and 'in jeopardy.' This bad news has meant: rising costs, double-digit premium increases, declining enrollment, carrier losses in the millions of dollars every year, increasingly stingy plans, and fewer carriers from which consumers can choose."

Consumers Flee Individual Market

The *Puget Sound Business Journal* reported in November 1997 that some 14,000 state residents had dropped their individual health insurance during the first half of the year. That followed an even steeper decline in 1996, when nearly 40,000 policyholders insured by the state's largest health insurers allowed their policies to lapse.

Through 1999, state legislators tried incrementally to address the problems caused by the 1993 law. With every adjustment, new problems arose. Even after a more conservative Legislature repealed some elements of the early legislation, major portions remained intact.

In September 1999, Dr. Pete McGough, medical director for Providence Health Center in Redmond, and Dr. George Schneider, part-time professor at Washington State University, wrote in the *Seattle Post-Intelligencer*, "Washington's health care financing mess will not blow over in a day, and the worst is yet to come. The financial burdens on doctors and hospitals, as they struggle to maintain full services with dwindling resources, pose a real threat to all Washington residents at all social and economic levels."

"By now," McGough and Schneider continued, "every major health insurance carrier has dropped out of the individual insurance market."

Group Health and Regence Blue Shield left, leaving individuals and families in 32 of the state's 39 counties without private individual insurance options. To make matters worse, officials for Basic Health Plan (BHP), the state-run "safety net," announced the plan would not accept new patients after January 2000. At the same time, State Sen. Pat Thibaudeau (D-Seattle) announced roughly 11 percent of the state's population was uninsured—about 600,000 residents, as many as were uninsured when the WHSA reform was adopted in 1993.

In 1994, roughly 790,000 individuals and families in Washington State were insured in the individual health insurance market. By 1998, the number had dropped to 530,000. (The figure has since climbed to 646,000 in 2003 as legislators adopted new reforms.)

Between 1993 and 2003, the number of Washington State residents insured by taxpayer-funded Medicaid increased by nearly 108 percent, from 405,000 in 1993 to 842,000 in 2003.

Before the WHSA, 30 insurers sold individual health insurance in Washington. Today there are seven: Premara Blue Cross, Regence Blue Shield, and Group Health Plan of Puget Sound (the three dominant providers), plus Regence Blue Shield of Idaho, Regence BCBS of Oregon, KPS Health Plan, and Premara Lifewise Health Plan.

High-Risk Response

Because no insurers were serving the market, in late 1999 Insurance Commissioner Senn reopened the state's high-risk health insurance pool to anyone seeking individual health insurance in counties with no private options. Because premiums for those enrolled in the pool were capped at 125 percent of average premiums if they chose the managed care option, and 150 percent of average if they chose the fee-for-service option, the risk pool was not an attractive option for those who did not have pre-existing health conditions.

In November 1999, a low-cost managed care plan was added to the risk pool for all counties where private insurance companies had been regulated out of business. Because most residents had access to that new low-cost option (32 of 39 counties had no private individual health insurance options, though people in counties bordering Idaho or Oregon were taken in by those respective state Blue Cross plans), and because the guaranteed issue mandate meant they could not be denied entrance to the pool, healthy consumers were encouraged to "game" the system by signing up for insurance only when they needed hospitalization, prescription drugs, or maternity care, exiting the pool when the medical event passed.

This created problems for the high-risk pool no different from those that had developed in the private health insurance market. For example, the April 5, 1996 issue of the *Wall Street Journal* reported, "A [Washington State] woman wrote to her insurance company congratulating them for their excellent maternity care while having her first baby. She had been uninsured, but signed up after she got pregnant. Now that her baby was born, she was canceling her policy, but assured the insurance company she would come back if she ever got pregnant again."

Road to Recovery

In 2000, Gov. Locke, determined to restore a competitive individual health insurance market, signed SB 6199, a bill that put Washington on the road to recovery. Under the new law:

- Insurers were allowed to return to risk-based underwriting. Persons who applied for individual health insurance but could not pass a health screening were allowed to apply for insurance in the high-risk pool;
- Premiums were still subject to modified community rating, but the insurance commissioner no longer had rating authority. Instead, the insurer had to meet a 72 percent loss ratio standard;
- The guaranteed issue mandate was adjusted to allow insurers to exclude coverage for pre-existing conditions for up to nine months; and
- An employee who loses his or her job through no fault of his or her own is entitled to guaranteed issue health insurance after all other sources (such as COBRA) are exhausted. Once those options are exhausted (or if the person had no such options to begin with), he or she has 63 days to sign up for an insurance policy, and that policy cannot be denied. This portability provision made Washington State law consistent with federal law.

Into the Future

The reform steps taken by Washington State policymakers in 2000 and 2004 have been in the right direction. Today, all counties report at least two insurers offering individual health insurance polices.

But, as the state's business groups and policy analysts have made clear, the state has a long way to go before it has undone the damage caused by the 1993 reform experiment.

6
Massachusetts

A proposed amendment to the Massachusetts state constitution, which would mandate that lawmakers provide medical insurance to all residents of the state, is the final stage in what critics have long warned would be a downward spiral for private health insurance caused by state over-regulation.

The amendment proposal, reported by the Associated Press on April 6, 2004, would require the state Legislature to "enact and implement such laws as will ensure that no Massachusetts resident lacks comprehensive, affordable, and equitably financed health insurance coverage for all medically necessary preventive, acute, and chronic health care and mental health care services, prescription drugs, and devices."

Dukakis' Play or Pay Plan
The proposed constitutional amendment is an attempt to address the unintended consequences of two decades of manipulation and over-regulation by state government of Massachusetts' insurance markets. The interference has left insurance rates high and consumers with only limited choices.

In the late 1980s, Massachusetts aimed to become the first state to create a single-payer health care system. The Universal Entitlement Act of 1988 was passed during an especially partisan time when the state's three-term governor, Michael Dukakis, was running for president.

Not unlike the Clinton administration's proposal to change the nation's health care system, the Dukakis plan tried to achieve universal coverage through an unfunded mandate on employers now called "play or pay." It required all businesses with 25 employees or more to provide health insurance as a benefit, or pay $1,680 per employee to a state pool from which uncovered workers could receive insurance.

The state's ambitious universal health care plan, however, was never put into place. Just as the Dukakis presidential bid was falling short, the state's economy was tanking. With state revenues plummeting and private employers battered by the economic downturn, there was neither the political will nor the financial wherewithal to put a health care-for-all plan into place. After repeated delays, the Universal Entitlement Act was officially repealed by the Legislature in 1995.

Over-Regulation in the 1990s and 2000

In 1996, the Massachusetts Legislature passed the Non-Group Health Insurance Reform Act (Massachusetts calls individual insurance "non-group"), which severely harmed the underwriting, pricing and marketing of individual and small group health insurance plans. Among the law's provisions:

- Insurers serving the Massachusetts small group market and insuring at least 5,000 persons (employees and dependents) were required to guarantee issue at least one product in the non-group market;
- The state division of insurance defined a standard individual insurance policy, specifying deductibles, premiums and coverage mandates for one HMO, one PPO and one indemnity-style plan. Insurers serving the individual insurance market were permitted to offer only the standardized plan in each category;
- Approved plans were required to offer annual open enrollment periods;
- Persons who were eligible for group coverage would not be eligible for non-group (individual) coverage;
- Rates could be modified from the state-established community rate only for age and geography. Rate variation for age was

extremely limited, ensuring that the young (with lower average incomes) subsidize the older population (with higher average incomes). Rates for plans with enhanced benefits could be adjusted to account for the benefit differences, but not for health risks; and

● Insurance premiums would have to be approved by the insurance commissioner. The cumbersome process imposed by the Legislature tied the rates of the insurer to its competitors' rates regardless of the experience of the carrier applying for the rate increase.

This law was virtually identical to New Jersey's 1992 law. Massachusetts academics Katherine Swartz, professor of health policy and management at the Harvard School of Public Health, and Deborah Garnick, professor at the Heller School for Social Policy and Management at Brandeis University, were both strong supporters of these measures and had championed their adoption in New Jersey. New Jersey officials testified before the Massachusetts Legislature in support of both guaranteed issue and community rating.

Legislation that passed in 2000 modified those rules in several ways. On the positive side, it allowed insurers to offer a second plan for individual insurance for HMO, PPO and indemnity-style coverage, subject to approval by the Division of Insurance. The rule that persons eligible for group coverage could not be eligible for individual coverage was repealed, and individual insurers were made to serve consumers eligible under HIPAA. A reinsurance pool (not a high-risk insurance pool) was established.

On the negative side, at least for insurance companies trying to offer individual health insurance in the state, the 2000 legislation changed the open enrollment mandate from once a year to continuous, with pre-existing conditions excludable by insurers for only six months. If the insured had prior coverage within 63 days of his or her new coverage, there is full portability—no pre-existing conditions could be excluded.

Individual Market Meltdown

The new insurance regulations in Massachusetts had predictable results. Two years after the 1996 legislation was adopted, approximately 20 health insurers stopped marketing plans in Massachusetts, according to industry observer Daniel Heystek, owner of Gramercy Insurance Brokerage in Arlington.

The new laws destroyed the individual insurance market. Among companies that left were such highly respected firms as Golden Rule Insurance Co., Travelers Insurance Companies, Mutual of Omaha, and Time Insurance Company. A few others did not leave but stopped underwriting individual policies.

On October 20, 2003, the *Boston Business Journal* noted not all of the departures were due solely to the new law: "Two big changes came after the Boston-based John Hancock Mutual Life Insurance Company sold its health plan to a California company, while Prudential Insurance Company auctioned off its insurance plan. But the new state law undoubtedly played a major role in forcing other players out of the market, industry observers say."

The stated aim of the Non-Group Health Insurance Reform Act was to make sure no one in Massachusetts would go uninsured. That goal was not realized. According to a report published in the March 26, 2004 issue of the *Boston Business Journal*, Blue Cross Blue Shield statistics, based on state reports, reveal that the number of uninsured persons in the state has increased from 365,000 in 2000 to more than 500,000 today.

High Insurance Premiums

The 2000 Medical Expenditure Survey, conducted by the Agency for Healthcare Research and Quality, finds Massachusetts to have the highest average annual premiums in the nation for family coverage through small group policies: $8,468. New Jersey comes in second at $8,274.

Individual insurance rates in the state are also high and, as a result, the share of persons insured in the state's individual insurance market fell from 10.8 percent in 1994 to 8.3 percent in 2003.

As of June 2005, monthly premiums in the state's non-group market ranged from $384 for a 25-year-old individual ($4,618 per year), offered by Fallon Community Health Plan Inc., to as high as $4,291 for the two-adult plan ($51,494 a year) offered by The MEGA Life Insurance Company. (See Massachusetts Figure 1.) Those rates are substantially higher than the national average annual premiums reported in the January/February 2004 issue of *Healthplan* magazine: $2,070 for single coverage and $4,009 for family coverage.

In an April 6, 2004 newswire report by the Associated Press, insurance broker Heystek said prior to the enactment of guaranteed issue and community rating he could have lined up coverage for a single 25-year-old at rates starting at $25 a month. "Premiums under many individual plans have since skyrocketed," said Heystek, "rising to more than $600 a month or more. It differs from company to company. For an individual to spend less than $180 a month is now the exception. It [guaranteed issue and community rating] has limited the choice."

The high cost of health insurance is the reason most often given by those who are uninsured. Yet Massachusetts policymakers, claiming to be concerned about the state's uninsured rate, nevertheless continue to support laws that increase the price of insurance.

Health Insurance for All?

With so much evidence available showing the failure of past attempts to regulate the state's private insurance market, what should Massachusetts' elected officials do? According to a coalition of liberal advocacy groups called the Health Care for Massachusetts Campaign, the solution is ... even more regulation! The group is the force behind the Health Care Insurance for Massachusetts Constitutional Initiative.

That proposal will be presented to the state's voters only if approved by the current Legislature and again by the new, two-year

Massachusetts Figure 1
Sample Monthly Premiums for Nongroup
Health Insurance in Massachusetts

Carrier	Status	Rate Offered in Boston
Aetna Life	Single	$820.19
	Family	$2,296.54
	Two Adults	$3,219.76
Aetna Health	Single	$493.87
	Family	$1,476.28
	Two Adults	$1,769.00
BCBS	Single	$503.29
	Family	$1,189.29
	Two Adults	$1,798.34
CIGNA - no longer offering		
Fallon	Single	$384.88
	Family	$1,206.65
	Two Adults	$1,300.27
The Guardian	Single	$527.51
	Family	$1,506.24
	Two Adults	$1,877.10
Harvard Pilgrim	Single	$396.94
	Family	$1,197.38
	Two Adults	$1,571.22
Health New England - not offered in Boston		
John Alden	Single	$675.22
	Family	$2,075.55
	Two Adults	$2,604.16
MEGA	Single	$1,110.67
	Family	$3,539.24
	Two Adults	$4,291.21
New England Life	Single	$653.96
	Family	$2,260.21
	Two Adults	$2,533.75
Tufts	Single	$538.76
	Family	$1,769.05
	Two Adults	$2,032.00
United Health	Single	$609.45
	Family	$1,930.49
	Two Adults	$2,419.58
United Healthcare	Single	$450.57
	Family	$1,427.13
	Two Adults	$1,775.16

Source: **http://www.mass.gov/doi/Consumer/css_health_Plans04_12.html**.
Rates are for December 1, 2004 to November 30, 2005.

Legislature that will take office in January 2005. The soonest the question could appear on the ballot, then, is November 2006.

The amendment's supporters say it will force lawmakers to come to grips with the state's health care crisis. Dr. Peter Slavin, president of Massachusetts General Hospital, told the Associated Press, "Some say we cannot afford the cost of covering the uninsured, but we are already paying for the much higher costs of failing to provide health care to those who need it."

Critics say the amendment would just extend to ridiculous and expensive extremes the failed policies of the past. Eileen McAnneny, vice president of government affairs for Associated Industries of Massachusetts, says the amendment could cost the state's taxpayers as much as $3 billion. Said Bill Vernon of the Massachusetts National Federation of Independent Business, "this amendment is not necessary. It is a statement of a goal that we all share ... but it doesn't get us any closer to that goal."

State Rep. William Galvin (D-Canton) warns, "If this becomes part of our constitution, the Legislature will be forced to come up with some solution and when they do, it's going to be taken to the SJC [Supreme Judicial Court] and the SJC is going to mandate it." Punting to the judiciary the difficult decisions about how to define, finance and deliver a major new public entitlement is hardly good public policy.

Better Alternatives

Other states have been more successful than Massachusetts in keeping health insurance premiums affordable, the uninsured rate low and the quality of health care services high. Policies they have adopted include:

- Establishing a high-risk health insurance pool for the medically uninsurable;
- Repealing guaranteed issue and community rating requirements, which would encourage insurers to re-enter the state by

discouraging behavior that leads to higher rates for everyone, but especially for younger and healthy consumers. The high-risk pool then acts as a safety net for those who cannot qualify for insurance;

- Repealing the cumbersome rate approval process that discourages price competition and offering consumers more choices;
- Allowing health insurers to offer "mandate-free" insurance polices to individuals and to small group plan sponsors; and
- Encouraging the use of Health Savings Accounts by giving public employees the option to choose them and providing state income tax deductions for deposits made to the accounts.

Conclusion

By now, state policymakers should know better than to propose more regulation as the solution to the state's health insurance woes. Rules and regulations already on the books have driven up prices and reduced consumer choices. More of the same kind of regulation will produce only more of the same results.

Much more promising than the constitutional initiative is a reform agenda that allows Massachusetts to take advantage of the trend toward consumer-directed health care. Competition among insurers and providers can lower prices and rationalize services; giving consumers choices can help them find the combination of price, service and financial risk that is best for them. Massachusetts needs to overcome its fear of markets if it ever hopes to achieve the goal of access to quality health care for all.

7
New Hampshire

On January 1, 2004, key provisions of a reform measure aimed at deregulating New Hampshire's small group health insurance market went into effect. The new law also affirmed reforms implemented two years earlier to the Granite State's individual medical market, allowing insurers to refuse to write or issue coverage based on an applicant's health status, medical underwriting for individual health coverage, and exclusion of pre-existing conditions for nine months (up from three months under previous law).

In testimony to the House Commerce Committee on April 23, 2003, Gov. Craig Benson (R) said, "SB 110 is a great step forward in the health care reform process. It will lower costs and give consumers choice by increasing competition among insurers."

How the Granite State came to see deregulation as the solution to the problems of rising health care costs and declining choices for consumers is a story worth telling, if only because policymakers in so many states still seem to think regulations are part of the solution rather than the cause of the problems.

Biggest Insurer Cried for Help

Benson's "great step forward" could also be described as a "great step backward," back to the time before the national debate over the failed Clinton Health Security Act and the poorly crafted reforms that New Hampshire and other states adopted in response to that debate.

In 1993, Blue Cross Blue Shield (BCBS) of New Hampshire (acquired by Anthem in 1999) began suffering financially from the guaranteed issue and community rating practices it was required by law to adopt. BCBS was the "insurer of last resort" in New Hampshire, and as such was more heavily regulated by the state than other insurers. In return, BCBS was exempted from paying the insurance premium tax (set at 2 percent of net premiums) levied on the rest of the state's private health insurance market. BCBS complained the guaranteed issue and community rating mandates made it unable to compete with firms permitted to use standard health insurance underwriting practices. Rather than seek freedom from the mandates, BCBS lobbied the New Hampshire Legislature to adopt rules that would force guaranteed issue and community rating on all state-regulated insurance companies.

"Despite having provider discounts no other carrier could match and favorable tax treatment to boot, BCBS was losing market share to other carriers," said Lee Tooman, vice president of Golden Rule Insurance Co. "Why? Because we had better products, prices and service. But Blue Cross prevailed in the Legislature, convincing elected officials that the problem was with us 'cherry pickers.'"

During the 1994 legislative session, Democrat Jeanne Shaheen, then a state senator, responded to BCBS by sponsoring SB 711, which passed and went into effect January 1, 1995. Among other provisions affecting the state's insurance industry, the measure:

- Required insurance companies to guarantee issue individual health insurance policies. Companies were prohibited from denying coverage to any person or eligible dependent;
- Imposed price controls, in the form of modified community rating, on individual health insurance premiums. Premiums could be modified or adjusted only for age, not health status; and
- Prohibited insurers from increasing premiums by more than 25 percent until January 2000.

Individual Insurance Market Imploded

Aimed primarily at easing the burden on BCBS by encumbering other insurers, Shaheen's SB 711 had no positive effect for health insurance consumers. According to the U.S. Census Bureau:

- In 1995, when SB 711 went into effect, 10.0 percent of the New Hampshire population was uninsured. In 2003, the uninsured rate stood at 10.3 percent;
- In 1995, 80.1 percent of the New Hampshire population had private health insurance. In 2003, 79.3 percent did; and
- In 1995, 9.8 percent of the New Hampshire population "directly purchased" health insurance, primarily in the individual market. In 2003, 7.1 percent did.

While health insurance coverage was little affected by Shaheen's reforms, consumer choice was badly damaged. By 1997, the number of commercial health insurers serving New Hampshire dwindled to five from a previous high of 12. Those remaining in the market reduced their insurance offerings to cover only high-deductible, catastrophic-type health insurance plans.

By 1997, even BCBS threatened to drop out of the individual health insurance market, complaining once again that its losses were unsustainable. The company followed through by quitting the state's market altogether and terminating all in-force business in January 1998.

The announcement "that [BCBS] would no longer participate in the individual market that they had done so much to define, heightened the growing concern of the remaining five carriers," testified attorney Paula Rogers on behalf of the Health Insurance Association of America at a hearing before the state insurance department on October 31, 1997.

"Since the Blue Cross Blue Shield announcement, we have seen our number of new policies issued in New Hampshire increase substantially," testified Cecil Bykerk, executive vice president and chief actuary for Mutual of Omaha. "We have also seen a significant increase in our anticipated loss ratio and this appears directly related to the influx of former Blue Cross Blue Shield policyholders. Our individual block of business, and indeed the entire remaining individual market in New Hampshire, is not broad-based enough to absorb the high claims costs associated with the Blue Cross Blue Shield block of business."

The New Hampshire Department of Insurance engaged the Washington, DC-based Center for Health Economics Research to investigate the effects of the Shaheen reform. The group's report, submitted on December 17, 1997, warned, "Blue Cross and Blue Shield's withdrawal from the nongroup [i.e., individual] market could lead to a market collapse if nothing is done to avoid a disorderly migration of this high-risk book to other insurers." Anthony Juliano, executive vice president of the Independent Insurance Agents of New Hampshire (IIANH), shared at the October 31 hearing the results of an IIANH membership poll on the availability of individual health insurance products after SB 711 was implemented. According to Juliano, "There was a significant reduction in the availability, and what was available was coming in with extra-high deductibles. It now appears that circumstances have not changed and are certain to worsen with the withdrawal of BCBS from the market."

Back to the Drawing Board

On November 26, 1997, the Department of Insurance issued a "Findings and Final Order" with respect to the condition of the state's individual health insurance market. Insurance Commissioner Charles Blossom found, among other things, that "the quality of products available in this market is worsening," "the cost of available products in this market is increasing," and "the loss ratios of the writing carriers has increased."

Blossom imposed a temporary risk-sharing plan, developed by the industry, to subsidize the losses experienced by the individual health insurance carriers. Insurers actively marketing in the individual market were eligible for a subsidy, paid for by assessments on all commercial insurance companies and HMOs.

The plan was widely perceived as necessary, but acceptable only as an interim measure. William Sterling, vice president and senior associate counsel for group insurance carrier John Alden, testified at the October 31 hearing, "The inability of a guaranteed issue, community rated individual health market to provide a sufficient, internal spread of risk and cost is apparent.

"The imposition of a risk-sharing plan by regulatory action is an acceptable and necessary solution to the problem at hand," noted Sterling. "However, at the earliest possible opportunity, a permanent solution should be sought through legislation."

Movement toward a legislative solution began in 1998. In legislation that went into effect July 1, 2002, the guaranteed issue requirement was repealed and a high-risk pool for the medically uninsurable launched. The measure also allowed for more flexibility in premium rating:

- Insurers were permitted to use medical underwriting to determine eligibility for insurance coverage and initial determination of rates;
- Premiums could be surcharged up to 50 percent for health status;
- Premiums could be surcharged up to 50 percent for smokers; and
- Premiums were permitted to vary for age by a factor of 4 to 1.

The New Hampshire high-risk pool, New Hampshire Health Plan (NHHP), is a cooperative state and private-sector insurance plan for the medically uninsurable. While eligibility under certain state and federal regulations immediately makes one eligible for NHHP, for the most part, enrollees must have been declined for private health insurance coverage and must have been diagnosed with one of 16 "pre-qualifying" medical conditions, among them HIV/AIDS, juvenile diabetes, multiple sclerosis and paraplegia/quadriplegia.

Two indemnity and two managed care options are offered through NHHP. Rates are higher for tobacco users than for those who do not use tobacco. Coverage is provided through private insurance companies at rates not higher than 150 percent, and not lower than 125 percent, of the standard market rate for the coverage offered.

Scot Zajic, a director for government relations at Assurant Health, said his company is a strong supporter of high-risk pools for persons who cannot get health coverage elsewhere. "Having a risk pool is a good way to provide access to health coverage for those who need it," Zajic said. "We would, however, like to see the funding base broadened to include federal and/or state funding. Finding coverage for medically uninsurable persons warrants a societal solution."

State of the Market Today

Zajic said two companies under the Assurant corporate umbrella serve the individual medical insurance market today: Fortis Insurance Co. and John Alden Life Insurance Co. "The recent reforms have allowed us to re-enter the New Hampshire market, and to offer more products that will benefit more consumers."

Golden Rule Insurance's Tooman disagreed with Zajic's assessment of competition in the state. "In 1994, Golden Rule had a thriving business in New Hampshire. We insured a lot of people and paid millions of dollars of claims expeditiously and accurately. But Blue Cross complained that carriers like Golden Rule were doing great harm in New Hampshire. In fact, the only entity suffering harm was Blue Cross.

"Jeanne Shaheen's 1994 reforms ended up freeing Blue Cross of its money-losing business and handed it a virtual monopoly in the individual market," Tooman continued. "Blue Cross returned to the individual market, able itself now to 'cherry pick.' But it still has the provider discounts no one else can touch.

"Ten years after 'reform,'" he said, "the market has not recovered."

8
Maine

In June 2003, Maine Gov. John Baldacci (D) signed the Dirigo Health Reform Act, creating a government-run, taxpayer-funded health insurance and medical care program for the state. Many have praised the initiative, which became effective in September of that year, as a bold effort to reform Maine's health insurance market.

But the individual and small group insurance markets in Maine had been in turmoil for more than a decade because of previous "bold efforts" to reform health insurance.

In 1993, the Maine Legislature imposed guaranteed issue and modified community rating on the individual insurance market in an effort to increase access to health insurance for the uninsured population. Specifically:

- Insurance premiums were not permitted to vary by gender, health status, claims experience or length of time with coverage. Insurers were permitted to adjust premiums by 20 percent more or less than the community rate for age, occupation, and geographic area, and premiums could be adjusted for smoking and family status; and
- Insurers were required to issue coverage to any applicant who had resided in the state for at least 60 days.

High and Rising Premiums

As is true with every other state to take this action, the mandates failed to make health insurance more affordable and accessible in Maine. Individual insurance premiums are well above the national average, ranging from hundreds of dollars per month for singles to thousands of dollars per month for families for plans with moderate deductibles. (See Maine Figure 1.)

"We know that Maine has the highest tax burden of all 50 states," wrote State Sens. Paul Davis (R-Sangerville) and Chandler Woodcock (R-Franklin) in a letter to the editor of the online newspaper The Daily ME, on March 11, 2004. "But do you also know that Maine has some of the highest health insurance [premium] rates?

"A Maine family of four buying an individual insurance policy from Anthem must pay $1,395 per month. And that's with a $1,000 deductible," Davis and Woodcock wrote. "Yet, that same family living across the border in New Hampshire only pays $586 a month for the same Anthem policy. If they live in the similarly rural state of North Dakota, then they only pay a low $346 per month.

"The reason for this difference is not hard to understand," the senators conclude. "It has to do with bad insurance regulation which drives up costs in Maine."

Maine Figure 1
Monthly Premiums for Standard Plan in Maine Individual Insurance Market (as of March 1, 2005)

Plan	Single	Two-Parent Family
Aetna Health	$1,015.21	$2,772.29
Anthem - Health Choice ($1,000 deductible)*	$526.59	$1,395.46
CIGNA Healthcare	$1,368.99	$3,760.06
Harvard Pilgrim	$1036.38	$3,109.15
HMO Maine (Anthem)	$1,011.29	$2,679.91

*Anthem also offers plans with lower and higher deductibles
All other plans in this table are HMO's without deductibles.
Source: Bureau of Insurance, Maine Department of Professional & Financial Regulation,
http://www.state.me.us/pfr/ins/indhlth.htm.

Fewer, More Expensive Choices

By some counts, half as many insurance companies serve the state's individual market as did so when the guaranteed issue and community rating laws were passed. Although five carriers—Aetna, Anthem (formerly Blue Cross Blue Shield), CIGNA, Harvard Pilgrim and Maine Partners Health Plans—write individual policies in Maine, the state is a virtual monopoly for Anthem, which in 2001 had 97.3 percent of the market, according to the Maine Bureau of Insurance.

Dave Spellman, president of Pratt Financial Group, Inc. in Westbrook, Maine and past president and legislative chair for the Maine chapter of the National Association of Insurance and Financial Advisors, noted, "I have seen first-hand the negative impact of over-regulation on insurance markets over the past 22 years of my career.

"Just over 10 years ago," he said, "we had well over 90,000 Maine consumers in the individual market. Today there are fewer than 30,000. From a competitive market with more than 10 carriers, we now have a monopolistic market with only one, Anthem, writing new individual policies."

Spellman pointed out, "While all this regulation was part of a stated overall goal to reduce insurance rates and, thereby, help decrease the ranks of the uninsured, just the opposite has occurred. Maine health insurance rates are now among the highest in America (two or three times that of just about anywhere else) and we have a growing uninsured population."

Adam Brackemyre, executive director of the Coalition Against Guaranteed Issue, agreed, saying: "Guaranteed issue and community rating have combined to accelerate Maine's health insurance costs above the national average."

Brackemyre cited a report issued in March 2004 by eHealthInsurance.com, a nationwide online health insurance business, which documented what its customers paid on average for individual coverage in 42 states representing 94 percent of the U.S. population. Maine was not included in the firm's survey. But customers in two other guaranteed issue and community rated states, New Jersey and New York, paid an average $335 a month for individual coverage. For all states, the average was $151 a month.

By contrast, the accompanying table (Maine Figure 1) shows rates for a standard plan in Maine range between $526.59 (Anthem's HealthChoice plan with a $1,000 deductible) and $1,368.99 per month for a single individual, and between $1,395.46 and $3,760.06 for a two-parent family.

R. Kenneth Lindell, a certified employee benefits specialist and Republican candidate for Maine House District 41, summed it all up when he wrote in the August 29 issue of the *Waldo County Citizen*, "Kentucky is a good case study because it made many of the same mistakes as Maine prior to enacting reforms in 2001.

"The result of these well-intended but misguided regulations," wrote Lindell, "was to force premiums higher, causing many to drop coverage and insurance companies to leave the state. By 2001, Kentucky's health insurance market was in chaos, with only one insurer [Anthem] left to cover the individual insurance market.

"If this story sounds familiar, it should. This is exactly what has happened in Maine in the last 10 years."

Little Improvement for Uninsured

Despite the chaotic market conditions, the uninsured rate in Maine has improved slightly, going from 11.1 percent of the state's population in 1993 to 10.4 percent in 2003, according to Census Bureau figures. But those figures mask a large movement of people from private insurance to public welfare programs.

While 16 percent of the state's residents were covered by individual policies in 1994 (figures for 1993 are not available), just 11 percent were covered in the individual market in 2003.

In 2003, 18 percent of the state's population was covered by Medicaid, up from 7.5 percent in 1995. "Little wonder," Spellman said, "why we have runaway income, sales, and property taxes and a budget deficit of over $1 billion."

High-Risk Pool

In 1990, Maine adopted one of the market-oriented reforms that have proven successful in other states: a high-risk pool for expanding access to the uninsured population. But the measure was short-lived. "The high-risk pool failed because enrollment was capped and the Legislature wouldn't fund it appropriately," said Spellman. "The pool was deemed a failure by the Democrat-controlled Legislature, so they came up with a final solution that destroyed the insurance market and brought us all closer to a single-payer health care plan with guaranteed issue and community rating."

Instead of a high-risk pool, the Legislature increased Medicaid eligibility, again with the goal of reducing the ranks of the uninsured. "Well," said Spellman, "that succeeded only in increasing the Medicaid population from just under 10 percent to over 20 percent of all Maine citizens. And the new Dirigo legislation could grow that population to 25 percent."

Voluntary Today ... Mandatory Tomorrow?

The insurance component of the Dirigo health plan, DirigoChoice, is a voluntary program for Maine residents who do not have coverage. Dirigo expected to enroll 31,000 people in 2004 and all 140,000 uninsured Maine residents within five years. At the beginning of 2005, only 1,800 had actually enrolled.

DirigoChoice will be available to uninsured Maine residents under age 65 whose income does not exceed 300 percent of the federal poverty level (about $55,000 for a family of four, $27,000 for an individual). The unemployed and self-employed will enroll in the plan as individuals with the benefit of heretofore unavailable group rates.

DirigoChoice also will be available to employees of small businesses in Maine, who will sign up through their workplaces. Participation by small businesses will be voluntary, government officials say.

But Arthur Levin, director of the New York-based Center for

Medical Consumers, says it is misleading to call participation in Dirigo "voluntary" for small businesses.

"Small businesses are going to get pressure from their employees to do this if they don't have insurance now. This plan calls for small businesses to pick up 60 percent for employees who work over 20 hours, and for their families," said Levin, adding, "This state is full of small businesses. This was a flawed plan from the get-go."

A Choice of One

Baldacci announced on August 23 that Anthem Blue Cross and Blue Shield of Maine—the insurer that already holds a near-monopoly on the state's individual insurance market—will administer DirigoChoice. The governor said marketing would begin October 1.

The DirigoChoice plan was supposed to be available at monthly community-rated premiums as low as $260 for a single adult and $780 for a family of four. The state planned to subsidize deductibles and out-of-pocket maximums and discount by up to 40 percent the monthly premiums incurred by enrollees under 300 percent of Federal Poverty Level.

Lee Tooman of Golden Rule Insurance Co. said, "Maine tried to contract with insurance carriers to sell subsidized health insurance to just about anyone. Since the carriers did not materialize, the state contracted with Maine Blue Cross." Meanwhile, the state will impose a new 4.1 percent tax on all health insurance premiums to finance universal health care.

In the first year, the plan predicts it will be paid for with $53 million in tax dollars set aside by the Legislature in 2003. In future years, the plan will be funded through a complex system of employer and employee payments, Medicaid cost-shifting, and a fee charged to insurers.

"A long time ago," Tooman said, "an actuary told me there are only two scenarios in which community rating works: Either you force people to buy the insurance or you subsidize it so heavily that people would be foolish not to buy it. Maine is going to try subsidies first. My guess is that this will not work and the next step will be an employer mandate, which would force employers to provide coverage."

"Maine is moving very fast toward government-run, single-payer health insurance," warned Scott K. Fish, director of special projects for the Maine Public Policy Institute. "The revised Maine Rx program is part of that movement. Maine's Dirigo Health Plan is another part."

"The governor and Legislature haven't learned a thing," said Merrill Matthews, director of the Council for Affordable Health Insurance. "Maine is next to Canada, and gets a lot of business from Canadians coming south of the border to get the medical care they can't get in Canada. With Dirigo, Canadians will still be traveling south, and Mainers will be joining them—heading to New Hampshire, or even further."

Resource Directory

Council for
Affordable Health Insurance
112 South West Street #400
Alexandria, VA 22314
Telephone 703/836-6200
mail@cahi.org
http://www.cahi.org

The Heartland Institute
19 South LaSalle Street #903
Chicago, IL 60603
Telephone 312/377-4000
Fax 312/377-5000
think@heartland.org
http://www.heartland.org

Association of
American Physicians & Surgeons
1601 North Tucson Boulevard #9
Tucson, AZ 85716-3405
Telephone 520/327-4885
Fax 520/325-4230
aaps@aapsonline.org
http://www.aapsonline.org

American Council on
Science and Health
1995 Broadway - 2nd Floor
New York, NY 10023-5860
Telephone 212/362-7044
Fax 212/362-4919
acsh@acsh.org
http://www.acsh.org

American Enterprise Institute
1150 Seventeenth Street NW
Washington, DC 20036
Telephone 202/862-5800
Fax 202/862-7177
jantos@aei.org
http://www.aei.org

American Legislative
Exchange Council
1129 20th Street NW #500
Washington, DC 20036
Telephone 202/466-3800
Fax 202/466-3801
info@alec.org
http://www.alec.org

The Josiah Bartlett Center
7 South State Street #2
Concord, NH 03301
Telephone 603/224-4450
Fax 603/224-4329
jbartlett@jbartlett.org
http://www.jbartlett.org/

The Beacon Hill Institute
Suffolk University
8 Ashburton Place
Boston, MA 02108-2270
Telephone 617/573-8050
Fax 617/994-4279
bhi@beaconhill.org
http://www.beaconhill.org/

Bluegrass Institute for
Public Policy Solutions
400 East Main Avenue #306
Bowling Green, KY 42102
Telephone 270/782-2140
Fax 305/675-0220
derry@bipps.org
http://www.bipps.org/

Cato Institute
1000 Massachusetts Avenue NW
Washington, DC 20001-5403
Telephone 202/842-0200
Fax 202/842-3490
mcannon@cato.org
http://www.cato.org

Citizens' Council on Health Care
1954 University Avenue West #8
St. Paul, MN 55104
Telephone 651/646-8935
Fax 651/646-0100
info@cchconline.org
http://www.cchc-mn.org

Coalition Against
Guaranteed Issue
112 South West Street #400
Alexandria, VA 22314
Telephone 703/837-1382
Fax 703/836-6550
mail@cagionline.org
http://www.cagionline.org

Coalition for
Affordable Health Coverage
1615 L Street NW #650
Washington, DC 20036
Telephone 202/626-8548
info@cahc.net
http://www.healthtaxcredits.org

Cornerstone Policy Research
136 North Main Street #2
Concord, NH 03301
Telephone 603/228-4794
Fax 603/228-6069
cornerstone@nhcornerstone.org
http://www.nhcornerstone.org

Empire Center for
New York State Policy
P.O. Box 7113
Albany, NY 12224
Telephone 518/434-3100
Fax 518/295-3130
ejm@empirecenter.org
http://www.empirecenter.org/

Ethan Allen Institute
4836 Kirby Mountain Road
Concord, VT 05824
Telephone 802/695-1448
Fax 802/695-1436
eai@ethanallen.org
http://www.ethanallen.org

Evergreen Freedom Foundation
P.O. Box 552
Olympia, WA 98507
Telephone 360/956-3482
Fax 360/352-1874
effwa@effwa.org
http://effwa.org

Galen Institute
P.O. Box 19080
Alexandria, VA 22320
Telephone 703/299-8900
Fax 703/299-0721
galen@galen.org
http://www.galen.org

The Heritage Foundation
214 Massachusetts Avenue NE
Washington, DC 20002-4999
Telephone 202/546-4400
Fax 202/546-8328
info@heritage.org
http://www.heritage.org

The HSA Coalition
2121 K Street NW #800
Washington, DC 20037
Telephone 202/271-3959
dperrin@hsainsider.com
http://www.hsainsider.com

Institute for Policy Innovation
1660 South Stemmons #475
Lewisville, TX 75067
Telephone 972/874-5139
Fax 972/874-5144
ipi@ipi.org
http://www.ipi.org

Maine Heritage Policy Center
P.O. Box 7829
Portland, ME 04112
Telephone 207/321-2550
Fax 207/773-4385
info@mainepolicy.org
http://www.mainepolicy.org/

Maine Public Policy Institute
27 State Street #68
Bangor, ME 04401
Telephone 207/944-3264
Fax 207/862-2433
betsy@maineinstitute.com
http://www.maineinstitute.com/

**Manhattan Institute for
Public Policy**
52 Vanderbilt Avenue
New York, NY 10017
Telephone 212/599-7000
Fax 212/599-3494
mi@manhattan-institute.org
http://www.manhattan-institute.org

**National Center for
Policy Analysis**
12770 Coit Road #800
Dallas, TX 75251
Telephone 972/386-6272
Fax 972/386-0924
devon.herrick@ncpa.org
http://www.ncpa.org

Pacific Research Institute
755 Sansome Street #450
San Francisco, CA 94111
Telephone 415/989-0833
Fax 415/989-2411
jgraham@pacificresearch.org
http://www.pacificresearch.org

Washington Policy Center
P.O. Box 3643
Seattle, WA 98124-3643
Telephone 888/972-9272
Fax 888/943-9797
info@washingtonpolicy.org
http://www.washingtonpolicy.org